The Colors of Christmas

A Musical for Senior Adult Choirs

Created and Arranged by MARTY PARKS

lillenas.com

Contents

A Festival of Carols

For Choir and Congregation

Arranged by Marty Parks

Joyful and Triumphant ♩ = ca. 94

Choir and Congregation

9 "Joy to the World" (ISAAC WATTS/GEORGE FREDERICK HANDEL)

13
earth re - ceive her King. Let
13 F G C
17
ev - 'ry heart pre - pare Him room, And
17 C/G
21
heav'n and na - ture sing, And heav'n and na - ture sing, And
21 C G G7

25
heav'n, and heav'n and na - ture sing.
28
C F6 C/G G7 C
CD: 2
O
C/B♭ F/A C/G F B♭m6/D♭ Csus C B♭/C
32 "O Come, All Ye Faithful" (JOHN F. WADE)
come, all ye faith - ful, joy - ful and tri -
F Gm7 F/A B♭ C Gm/B♭ F2/A Gm F C/E B♭

36
um - phant. O come ye, O come ye to
F/C A7/C♯ Dm 36 G6/B G7/B C Dm C/E F
40
Beth - le - hem. Come and be -
C/G G N.C. 40 FM7 Gm/F F
CD: 3
O
hold Him– born the King of an - gels!
O
O
B♭/F C7/F F C/E F G9/B G C Csus C F

44
come, let us a - dore Him!
come,
come, let us a - dore Him! O come, let us a -
O come,
O come,
44
F C F/C C7 F/C C F/C C7
48
dore Him! O come, let us a - dore Him–
F/C C F 48 Gm F C/E G7/D C C/B♭ F/A B♭
51
CD: 4
Christ, the Lord!
F/C C7 B♭/C 51 F F/E♭ B♭/D B♭ C/G

"Angels, from the Realms of Glory" (JAMES MONTGOMERY/HENRY T. SMART)
55
mf
An - gels, from the realms of glo - ry,
F sus
F
B♭
B♭2
mf
Wing your flight o'er all the earth.
59
Ye who sang cre - a - tion's sto - ry,
E♭/B♭
B♭
F/B♭
D/F♯
Now pro - claim Mes - si - ah's birth.
63
f
Come and wor - ship.
Gm
D/A
Gm/B♭
G°/D♭
F/C
C
F

Come and wor - ship. Wor - ship Christ, the new - born King.
B♭ D∅7 E♭ Cm B♭/D E♭6 Gm Fsus F7 B♭
CD: 5
69
"Angels We Have Heard on High" (Traditional French Carol)
Glo - - - ri - a in ex - cel - sis De - o!
A♭/B♭ B♭ B♭/C Csus
N.C.
F/A C F B♭ F/C C

75
Glo - - - ri - a
75 N.C.
79
CD: 6
in ex - cel - sis De - o!
79 G/B D G C G/D D G G/D F/D G
82 Choir only
In ex - cel - sis De - o!
82 G/B D G C D7sus D7 G G/D F/D G G/D F/D G F/D G

NARRATOR: Tonight [today] we gather to prepare for the birthday of a King; to make ready our welcome for the Son of God, Jesus the Messiah. And as we celebrate this joyful and holy season, we adorn this, His sanctuary, with symbols that remind us of His birth, His life, His sacrifical death and His triumphant resurrection.

"For God so loved the world that He gave His one and only Son, that whoever believes in Him shall not perish but have eternal life." *(John 3:16)*

So, let the celebration begin!

Deck the Halls

KEN BIBLE
and Traditional

Welsh Melody
Arranged by Marty Parks

11
'Tis the sea - son to be jol - ly,
Fa la la la la, la
11
D A7/C♯ D A7 Bm A D A D G6
la la la.
15
Fill the world with sounds of Christ - mas,
D/A A7 D
15
A A7 D A/C♯
Fa la la la la la, la la la.
19
Sing, for God Him -
D Dsus/E D/F♯ Bm/D F♯/C♯ Bm A/E E7 A
19
D A7/C♯ D A7

self is with us! Fa la la la la, la la la la.
Bm A D G D G6 D/A A7 D
23
CD: 8
23
G D G D G D D/A A7
mf
f
27
Alto solo
mf
See the Ho - ly Child be - fore us,
Choir
f
Fa la la la la, la
D N.C. A D G6

31
la la la.
Tenor solo
mf
Rise and join the an - gel cho - rus,
D/A A7 D
31
D N.C.
mf
CD: 9
Choir
f
35
Duet
f
Fa la la la la, la la la la.
God is good be -
f
f mel.
A D G6 D/A A7 D
35
N.C.
f
Choir
yond all mea - sure! Fa la la la la la, la la la.
D Dsus/E D/F♯ Bm/D F♯/C♯ Bm A/E E7 A

39
Duet
Choir
Gave us ev - er - last - ing trea - sure! Fa la la la la, la
39
D
N.C.
G
D
G6
la la la. Fa la la la la, Fa la la la la,
43
Duet
D/A
A7
D
G
D
G6/D
D
Choir
Fa la la la la, la la la la.
G
D
G6
D/A
A
N.C.
3

NARRATOR: At Christmas we adorn our sanctuary and our homes with evergreens because they don't die or change color, even in winter. Their rich green color represents renewal, freshness and rebirth. *(music begins)* They remind us of the rich, abundant life in Jesus Christ…a life that will never fade and never die.

O Christmas Tree!

with

Immanuel, Immanuel

Traditional
and MARTY PARKS

German Folk Song
Arranged by Marty Parks

14
ver - dant green your branch - es. In sum - mer's heat or
Fm7/A♭ C/G Fm B♭7 E♭2 4 E♭
14
E♭ A♭/E♭ E♭
win - ter's chill, You show your Mak - er's per - fect skill. O
B♭7 Cm7 B♭7/D A♭/E♭ E♭
18
Christ - mas tree, O Christ - mas tree! How ver - dant green your
18
E♭ B♭ E♭ G7/D C Fm/A♭ C/G Fm B♭7

CD: 11
branch - es.
O
E♭4/2
E♭
Fm/A♭
C/G
Fm
Fm/A♭
B♭sus
B♭
24
Christ - mas tree,
O
Christ - mas tree!
You
point to God in
E♭
B♭
E♭
Fm7/A♭
C/G
Fm
B♭7
heav - en.
O Christ - mas tree,
O Christ-mas tree!
You
28
E♭4/2
E♭
B♭
E♭

32
point to God in heav - en. Re - mind - ing us we
Fm7/A♭ C/G Fm B♭7 E♭2 4 E♭
32 E♭ A♭/E♭ E♭
need not fear, For God has cho - sen to draw near. O
B♭7 Cm7 B♭7/D A♭/E♭ E♭
36
Christ - mas tree, O Christ - mas tree! You point to God in
36 E♭ B♭ E♭ G7/D C Fm/A♭ C/G Fm B♭7

22
CD: 12
*"Immanuel, Immanuel"
With strength
heav - en. Im - man - u-el, Im -
man - u-el, Al - might-y God is with us! Im - man - u-el, Im -
man - u-el, Al - might-y God is with us. The Lord of heav - en

high a - bove Has come to us in ten - der love. Im -
F/C C7 Dm7 C7/E B♭/F F N.C.
8vb
54
man - u - el, Im - man - u - el, Al - might - y God is
F C F A7/E D Gm/B♭ D7/A Gm C7
58
rit.
with us!
F4/2 F Gm/B♭ D7/A Gm C7 F4/2 F
rit.

NARRATOR: "In the beginning was the Word, and the Word was with God and the Word was God. He was with God in the beginning. He was in the world, and though the world was made through Him, the world did not recognize Him. He came to that which was His own, but His own did not receive Him. Yet to all who received Him, to those who believed in His name, He gave the right to become children of God. *(John 1:1,2,10-12)*

Jesus Himself said, "Everyone who looks to the Son and believes in Him shall have eternal life. *(music begins)* I tell you the truth, he who believes has everlasting life. *(John 6:40, 47)*

All Year Long

Words and Music by
BOB FARRELL
Arranged by Marty Parks

yule - tide song, or the gifts that we hold so dear; But
Dm
B♭M9
F
C7
C♯°7
Dm
B♭M7
CD: 14
rit.
14
Brightly in 2 ♩. = ca. 62
yes, it's the rea-son for cheer!
F2/C
C
C7
F
Am/C
Gm/C
Am/C
Gm/C
F
rit.
Brightly in 2
mf
cresc.
Choir
f
18
Im - man - u - el, ring the bells, Keep them
f
Am/C
18
F2
C6/E
f
8vb

22
ring - ing all year long. Im-man-u - el, hear those bells, They're pro-
B♭M9 Gm C
22
F2
C6/E
26
claim - ing all year long: "Glo - ry to God in the
B♭M9 Gm Csus C
26
F Gm
CD: 15
high - est, Peace on earth!"
F/C C2 B♭/C F B♭M9 F/C C F

mf
32
The King, wrapped in swad-dling lives on to-day, He
mf
E♭sus
E♭
A♭
F m
36
reigns in the hearts of men;
The won-der of Christ-mas is
C m
B♭m9
CD: 16
born ___ with-in by re-ceiv-ing the pres-ent He gave.
Let's
D♭
A♭/E♭
D♭M9

40
cel - e-brate Je - sus each day!
Im - man - u -
A♭/E♭
E♭
A♭
C sus
C6
43
el, ring the bells, Keep them ring - ing all year
F2
C6/E
B♭M9
Gm
long. Im - man - u - el, hear those bells, They're pro -
C
47
F2
C6/E

51
CD: 17
claim - ing all year long:
"Glo - ry to God in the
B♭M9 Gm Csus C
51 F Gm
high - est, Peace on earth!"
Im-man-u - el!
55
Ring those
Ring those
F/C C2 B♭/C F C6
55 F6
bells; they're ring - ing all year long.
bells, keep them ring - ing all year long. Im - man - u -
C/E C6/E B♭2 Gm7 C7 C6

59
Hear those bells pro - claim - ing
el, hear those bells, They're pro - claim - ing all year
59
F6
C/E
C6/E
B♭2
Gm7
all year long:
long:
63
"Glo - ry to God in the high - est, Peace on
C7sus
C7
63
F
Gm
F/C
C2
B♭/C
ff
earth!"
Im - man - u - el!
ff
F
Dm
Gm7
Csus
N.C.
ff

NARRATOR: The poinsettia is perhaps the most popular of all Christmas flowers. Its red leaves are said to represent the blood of the male infants King Herod had slain, and their star shape is said to symbolize the star that stood over the Christ Child. No wonder the poinsettia has been called the Flower of the Holy Night.

Mostly, the red we see in poinsettias, holly berries and ribbons symbolizes the blood Jesus shed for the forgiveness of our sins. You see, the Babe in the manger is also the Lamb of God who takes away the sins of the world. For centuries the earth had longed for a Savior, a Messiah, One who would redeem and save. *(music begins)* And then, just as the prophets had foretold, He came.

Earth Was Waiting

W. C. SMITH

MARTY PARKS
Arranged by Marty Parks

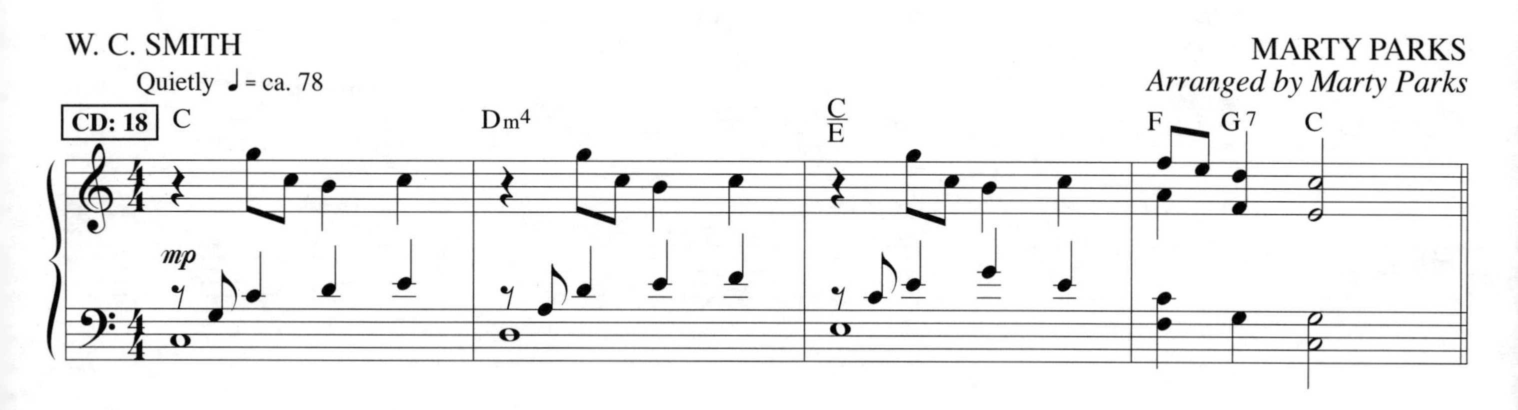

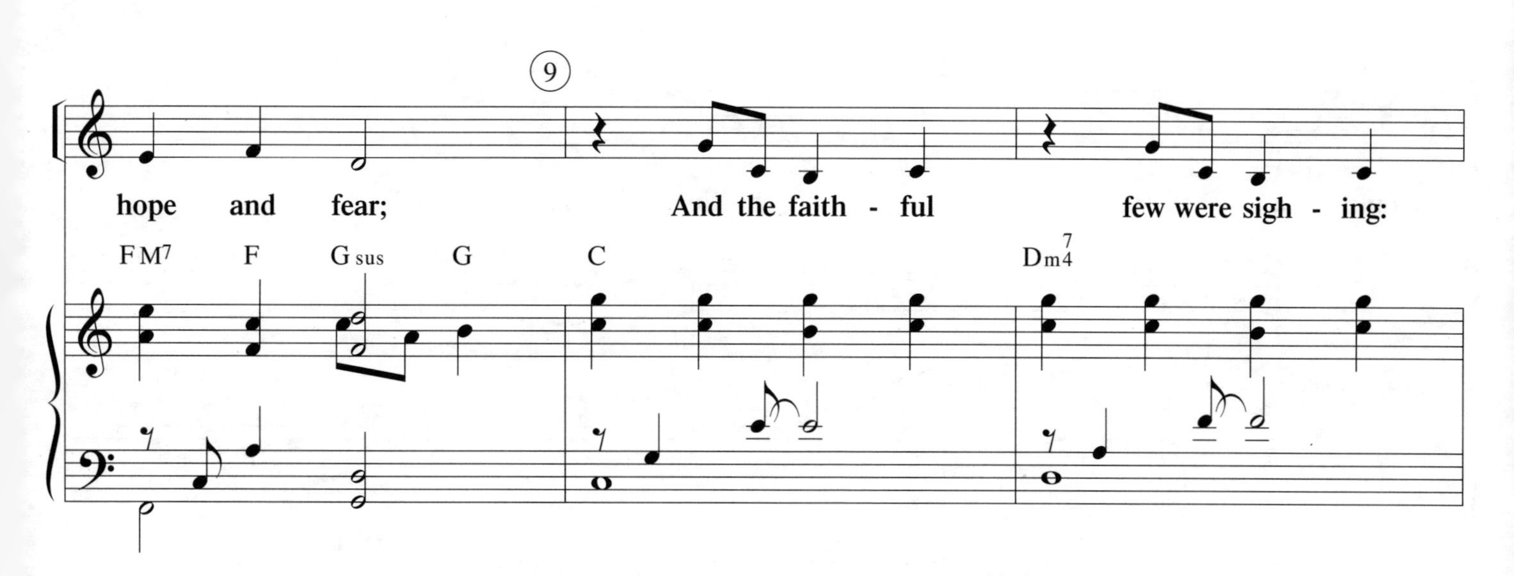

"Sure - ly Lord, the day is near.
C/E
F
G7
C
E/B
13
mf
The De-sire of all the na - tions, It is time He
mf
13
Am
Em7
F/A
G
F/C
C
Am
Em7
mf
should ap - pear.
17
mp
It is time He should ap - pear."
mp
F
G
Asus
A
17
Dm7
G9
C
mp

CD: 19
Dm4
C
E
F
G7
C
22
Then the Spir - it of the High - est on a vir - gin
22
N.C.
26
meek came down;
And He bur - dened her with bless - ing,
26

And He pained her with re - nown.
N.C.
F
G7
C
E
B
30
For she bore the
For she bore the
Lord's a - noint - ed,
Am
Em7
F
A
G
F
C
C
mf
For His cross and
For His cross and
for His crown.
Am
Em7
F
G
Asus
A

34
For His cross and for His crown.
34
Dm7
G9
C
C/B♭
CD: 20
39
With strength
f
Earth for Him had
G/A
A sus
A 7
39
D
cresc.
f
groaned and wait - ed
since the a - ges
first be - gan;
Em7/4
D/F♯
G M7
G
A sus
A

43
For in Him was hid the se - cret that thro' all the
43
D
Em4 7
D/F♯
a - ges ran–
47
Son of Ma - ry,
G
A7
D
F♯/C♯
47
Bm
F♯m7
Son of Da - vid, Son of God and
G/B
A
G/D
D
Bm
F♯m7

51
mf
Son of Man.
Son of God and Son of
G
A
B sus
B
Em7
A9
CD: 21
54
mp
Man.
Son of God and
D
Bm7
Em
D
E
rit.
Son of Man.
Em
A
A13
G
D
D2

NARRATOR: "When the time had fully come, God sent His Son, born of a woman, born under law, to redeem those under the law, that we might receive the full rights of sons." *(Galatians 4:4, 5)* "For God did not send His Son into the world to condemn the world, but to save the world through Him." *(John 3:17)* "Thanks be to God for His indescribable gift!" *(2 Corinthians 9:15)*

On This Day Earth Shall Ring

Piae Cantiones
tr. by JANE M. JOSEPH
alt. by MARTY PARKS

MARTY PARKS
Arranged by Marty Parks

CD: 23
13
Him who the Fa - ther gave us.
13 Dm Dm/C B♭ C C7 F F
F 17 F2/A B♭ C
17
By the star o - ver His head,
Wise men three were to Him led;
21
Kneel - ing low there be -
Kneel - ing be -
F F2/A B♭ C 21 A/C♯ Dm

CD: 24
side His bed;
side His bed; There to praise and a - dore Him,
C F Gm C C/B♭ A A7/C♯
They lay their gifts be - fore Him.
27
Al -
Dm Dm/C B♭ C C7 F B♭
- le - lu - ia!
31
Glo -
C/B♭ B♭ Am Dm Gm

ry to God!
C6 C F2/A F
35
Al - le - lu -
35 B♭ C/B♭ B♭ A A/C♯
ia! Glo - ry to
39
Dm 39 Gsus G2 G

CD: 25
God!
C sus
C
D sus
45
On this day an - gels sing,
D
G
G2
B
C
D
With their song the earth shall ring,
49
Prais - ing Christ our
B
D♯
Em

heav'n - ly King, Born on earth to save us,
D G Am D D/C B B7/D♯
53
Peace and love He gave us.
Em Em/D C D D7 G Em Em/D C
cresc.
ff
Glo - ry to God!
Dsus D G

Jesus, Jesus, Rest Your Head

Solo

American Folk Song
Arranged by Marty Parks

rit.
13
a tempo
at their birth. Je - sus, Je - sus, rest Your head,
D9/F♯ Gsus G7 C Am7 FM7 Gsus G
rit.
a tempo
CD: 27
You have got a man - ger bed.
C Am7 Dm G7 C2
19
mf
Have you heard a - bout our Je - sus?
C2 Am Em/G F Esus E
mf
23
Have you heard a - bout His fate? How His moth - er
Am Em7/G Bm/F♯ G Am Am Em/G

went to the sta - ble on that Christ - mas eve so late?
F Esus E Am Em7/G Bm/F♯ G Am
27
CD: 28
Winds were blow - ing, cows were low - ing; Stars were glow - ing,
F F2 C C4/2 C F C/E
rit.
31
a tempo
mp
glow - ing, glow - ing. Je - sus, Je - sus, rest Your head,
Dm Gsus G C Am7 FM7 Gsus G
rit.
a tempo
mp
35
You have got a man - ger bed. All the e - vil
C Am7 FM7 Gsus G F C/E

(,)
rit.
folk on earth sleep in feath - ers at their birth.
Dm G7/B C2 F C/E D9/F♯ Gsus G7
rit.
39
a tempo
Je - sus, Je - sus, rest Your head, You have got a
C Am7 FM7 Gsus G C Am7
a tempo
45
p
man - ger bed. You have got a
Dm G7 C2 Am7 F FM7
p
(,)
man - ger bed.
G7sus G7 C2 C2 C

NARRATOR: Candles and the light they display remind us that Jesus is the Light of the World. He is the only true hope for our sin-darkened lives. In fact, light is the ideal metaphor for Christ. His presence, like even the tiniest candle flame, dispels the darkness and spills over into a dreary world. As we let the love of Christ shine through us, we illuminate all those we come in contact with. And just as a room full of candles produces a blazing glory, *(music begins)* so when we join the light of other believers, we light up the world with the love of Christ.

O Little Town of Bethlehem

PHILLIPS BROOKS
Tenderly ♩ = ca. 80

LEWIS H. REDNER
Arranged by Marty Parks

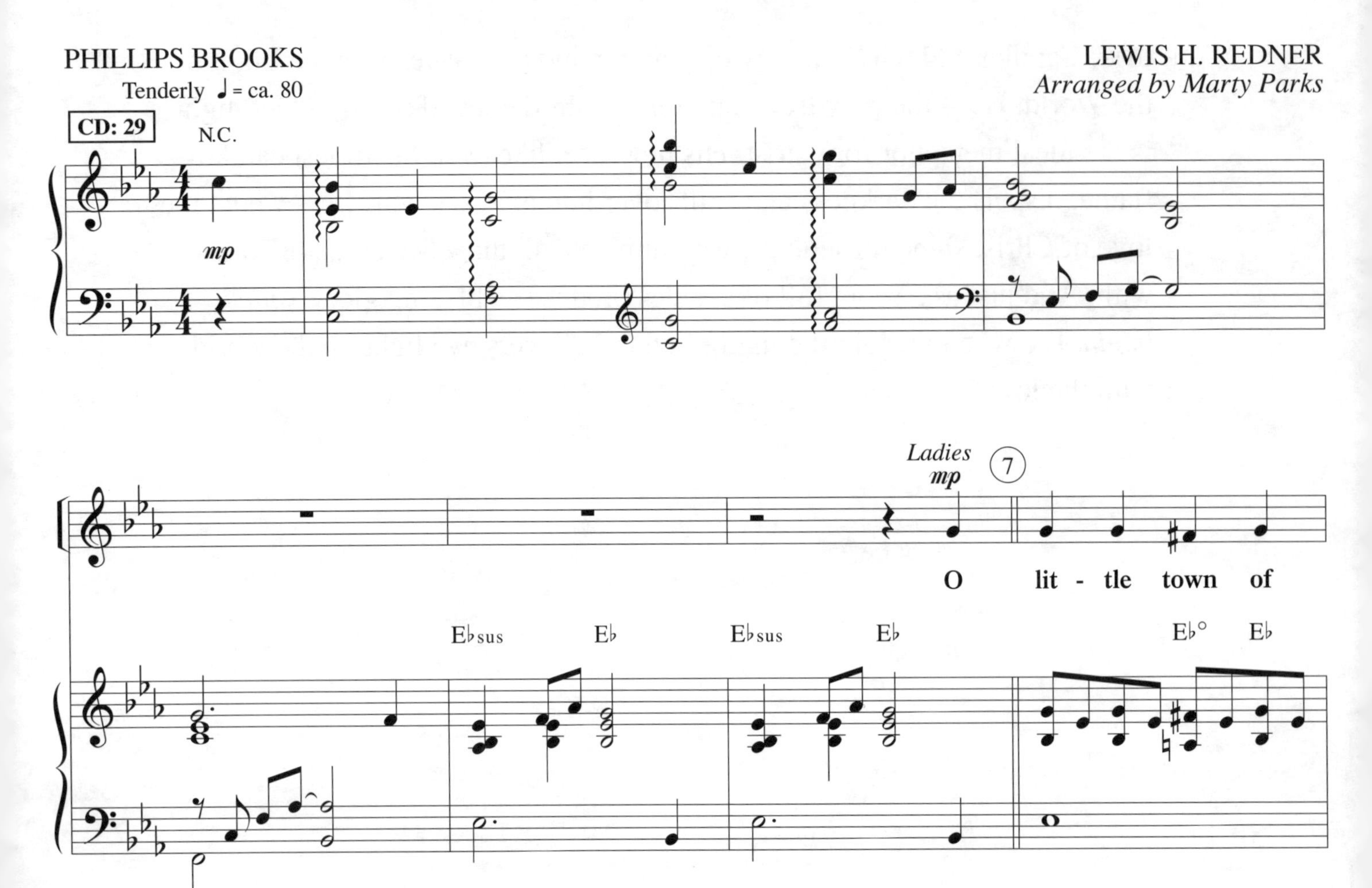

11
CD: 30
bove thy deep and dream - less sleep The si - lent stars go
E♭ E♭2/D♭ C C7 F7sus Fm7 E♭/B♭ B♭6 9 B♭
mf
15
by. Yet in thy dark streets shin - eth The ev - er - last - ing
E♭ D°/F A°/F♯ G G7 Cm Fm6/C Cm Fm/C
19
Light; The hopes and fears of all the years Are
G E♭ E♭° E♭ C+/A♭ Fm/A♭ Fm Fm/A♭

23
CD: 31
met in thee to - night.
E♭/B♭
A°/B♭
B♭9/6
B♭
E♭
23
E♭/D♭
Ladies
mp
27
How si - lent - ly, how
C sus
C
F
F°
F
decresc.
mp

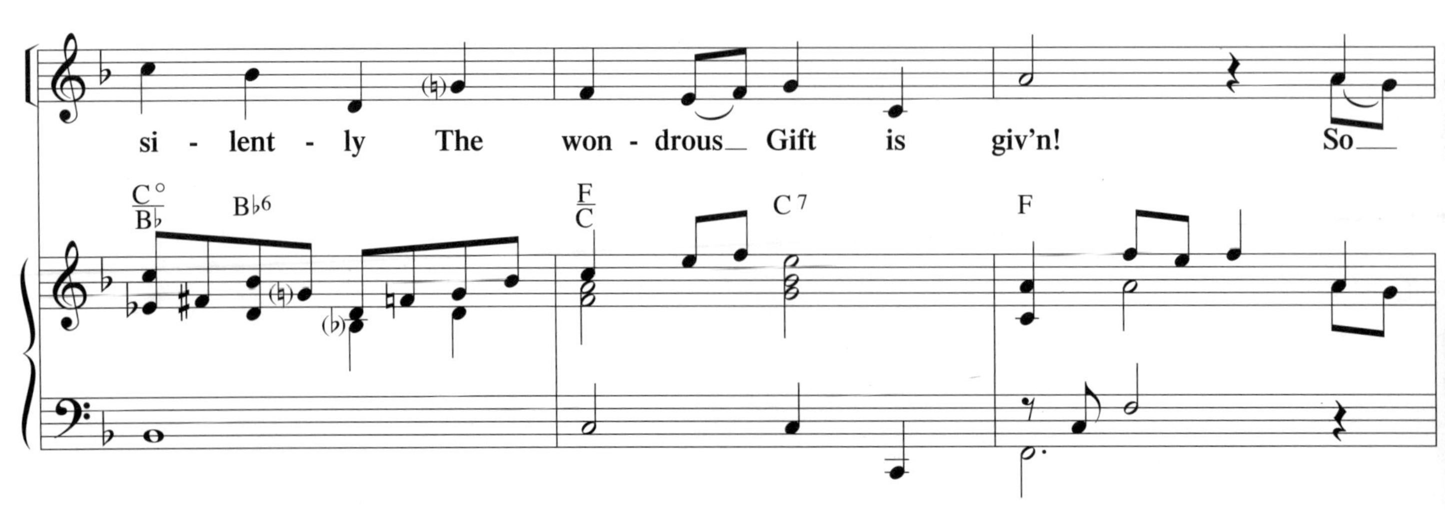
si - lent - ly The won - drous Gift is giv'n! So
C°/B♭
B♭6
F/C
C7
F

31
CD: 32
God im - parts to hu - man hearts The bless - ings of His
F
F2/E♭
D
D7
G7sus
Gm7
F/C
C9/6
C
mf
35
heav'n.
No ear may hear His com - ing; But
A7
A
E°/G
B°/G♯
39
in this world of sin, Where meek souls will re -
Dm
Gm6/D
Gm/D
F°

mp
ceive Him still, The dear Christ en - ters in. Oo,
mp
D+/B♭ Gm/B♭ Gm Gm/B♭ F/C B°/C C9/6 C F N.C.
mp
43
Oo,
43
46
rit.
Oo.
46
rit.

NARRATOR: "The people walking in darkness have seen a great light; on those living in the land of the shadow of death a light has dawned. For to us a child is born, to us a son is given, and the government will be on his shoulders. And he will be called Wonderful Counselor, Mighty God, Everlasting Father, Prince of Peace." *(Isaiah 9:2,6)*

Jesus the Lord Is Born

MARTY PARKS

Czech Folk Tune
Arranged by Marty Parks

17
Bright - er than an - y star up in heav-en, Je - sus the Lord is born!
D G/D D G/D D A D A
21 Ladies
Shep - herds a - dore Him, Bow - ing be - fore Him;
An - gels are sing - ing,
21 D(no 3) A D(no 3)
25
Je - sus the Lord is born!
Prais - es are ring - ing;
D(no 3) A 25 D A7 D N.C.
mp

CD: 36
29
D
E♭
A♭2/E♭
B♭
mf
33
God's on - ly Son is laid in a man - ger, Je - sus the Lord is
Born, He is born! Je - sus is
A♭/E♭
37
born! Born, He is born! Je - sus is
born! Com - ing to earth a Child and a Strang - er, Je - sus the Lord is

41
born!
born!
Wise men are prais-ing, Their voic-es rais-ing;
E♭
B♭
41
E♭(no 3)
B♭
45
Bring - ing their trea-sure, Great is its mea-sure;
Je - sus the Lord is
E♭(no 3)
B♭
45
E♭
B♭7
49
born!
E♭
N.C.
mp
49
F
B♭2
F
f

CD: 37
53
Choir
f
Come, see the Light in
F
B♭2
F
F
C
F
B♭
F
Beth - le - hem shin - ing, Je - sus the Lord is born!
F
B♭
F
F
C
F
57
Love of our Heav'n - ly Fa - ther de - fin - ing, Je - sus the Lord is
F
B♭
F
F
B♭
F
F
C
61
Ladies
born! Come and a - dore Him, Bow down be - fore Him;
F
C
F(no 3)
C

65
Come with your sing - ing, Your prais - es ring - ing; Je - sus the Lord is
F(no 3)
C
65
F
C7
CD: 38
69
f
born!
Je - sus the
f
F
N.C.
mp
F
F
C
69
F
f
Lord is born!
C
C7
F
B♭
F
F
B♭
F
F

NARRATOR: Tonight [today] we have celebrated the birth of Jesus Christ by singing the music of Christmas. We have adorned His sanctuary with symbols that remind us of Him. Our prayer for each of you is that His love, His life and His light will be a very real part of your day to day living, not just at this season, but forever!

Merry Christmas, everyone!

Finale

includes
Arise, Shine
Lift Up Your Heads
O Come, Let Us Adore Him

Arranged by Marty Parks

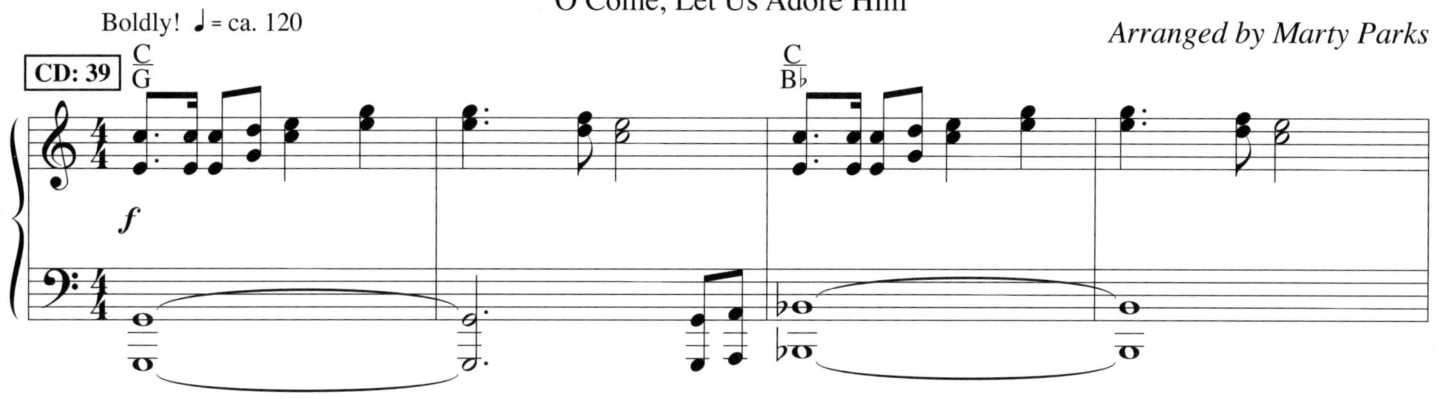

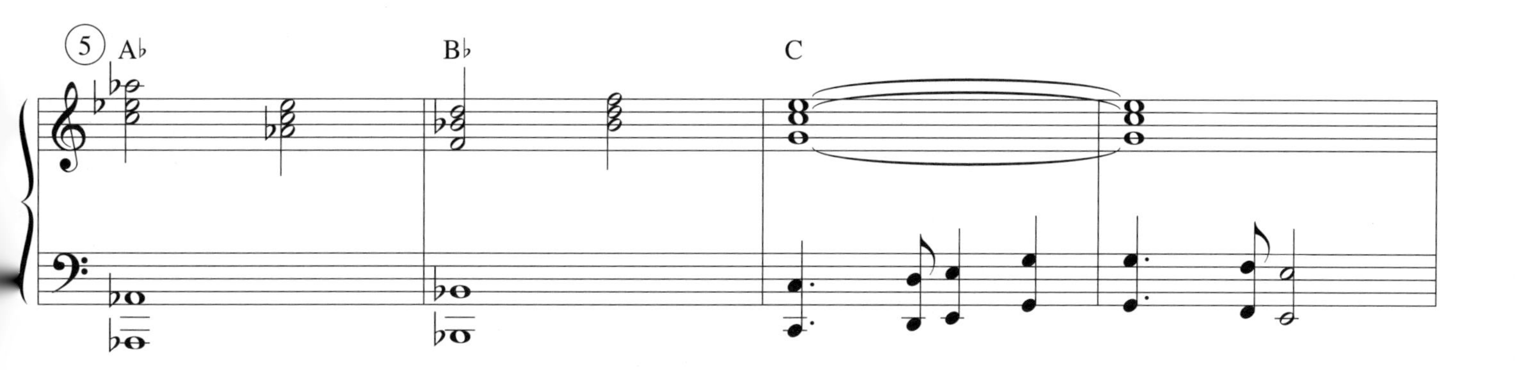

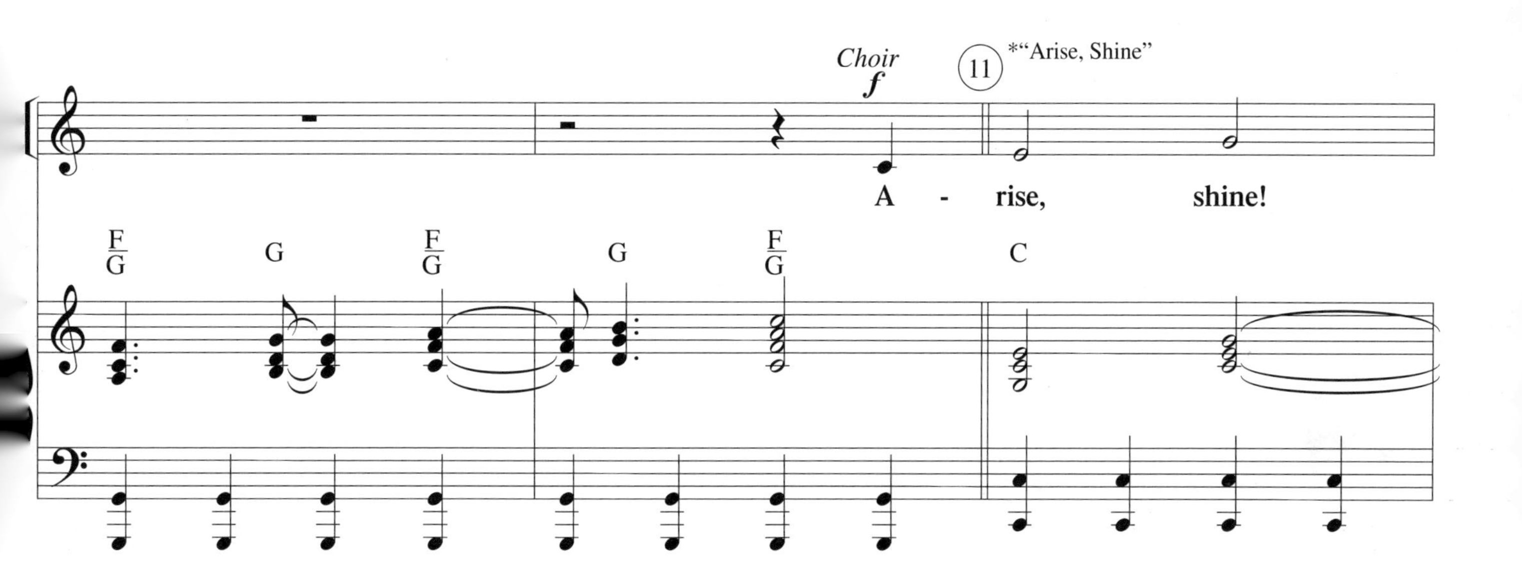

*Words and Music by STEVEN URSPRINGER and JAY ROBINSON.

For your Light is come. A-
C F/C C B♭ F
15
rise, shine! For your Light is come.
C F/C C
19
And the glo-ry of the Lord is ris-en, The
C F FM7 Em7 Dm7 C/E
23 CD: 40
glo-ry of the Lord is come; The glo-ry of the Lord is
F FM7 Em7 Am Am/G F FM7 Em7

27
ris-en up-on you!
And the glo-ry of the Lord is
Dm7
F/G G7
C
27
F
FM7 Em7
ris-en, The glo-ry of the Lord is come; The
Dm7
C/E
F
FM7 Em7
Am
Am/G
31
CD: 41
glo-ry of the Lord is ris-en up-on you!
31
F
FM7 Em7
Dm7
F/G G7
C

35
*"Lift Up Your Heads"
Lift up your heads
to the com - ing King.
39
Bow be-fore Him
and a-dore Him; sing.
Bb/C C7 F C/G F/A Bb Gm7
C Bb/C C7 F Eb/F F7
Bb C/Bb F/A Csus/G C C7

43
To His Maj - es - ty let your prais - es
F C/G F/A B♭ Gm7 C B♭/C C7
be– Pure and ho - ly, giv - ing glo - ry
47
F E♭/F F7 B♭ C/B♭ B♭
to the King of Kings. To the
51
CD: 42
Gm7 Dm7 Csus C B♭/C F Gm7 Dm7

rit.
King of Kings! O
C7sus C7 B♭2/C F F/E♭ Dsus D C/D
rit.
55
*"O Come, Let Us Adore Him"
Slower ♩ = ca. 80
come, let us a - dore Him, O come, let us a -
G D/G G D/G G G D/F♯ G C
59
CD: 43
dore Him; O come, let us a - dore Him–
G/D D G Am G/B C6 Em/C♯ D D/C G/B Am7
8vb

63
Christ the Lord! His Light will shine for - ev - er, His Light will shine for - ev - er; His
67
Light will shine for - ev - er, Christ the
CD: 44
G/D D7 C/D G E♭ D♭/E♭
A♭ E♭/A♭ A♭ E♭/A♭
A♭ E♭/G A♭ D♭ A♭/E♭ E♭ A♭
B♭m A♭/C D♭6 Fm/D E♭ E♭/D♭ A♭/C B♭m7 A♭/E♭ E♭7 D♭/E♭
8vb

71
Lord!
A - rise!
A♭
B♭/A♭
A - rise,
and
C♭/A♭
E♭7
76
shine!
N.C.